COPING WITH
GENDER
DYSPHORIA

Ellen McGrody

New York

Published in 2018 by The Rosen Publishing Group, Inc.
29 East 21st Street, New York, NY 10010

Copyright © 2018 by The Rosen Publishing Group, Inc.

First Edition

Expert Reviewer: Jan Hittelman, PhD

Library of Congress Cataloging-in-Publication Data

Names: McGrody, Ellen, author.
Title: Coping with gender dysphoria / Ellen McGrody.
Description: First edition. | New York, NY : Rosen Publishing, 2018. | Series: Coping | Audience: Grades 7-12. | Includes bibliographical references and index.
Identifiers: LCCN 2017005822 | ISBN 9781508173915 (library bound)
Subjects: LCSH: Gender identity disorders—Juvenile literature.
Classification: LCC RC560.G45 M35 2018 | DDC 616.6/94—dc23
LC record available at https://lccn.loc.gov/2017005822

Manufactured in the United States of America

CONTENTS

INTRODUCTION

The cultural and political landscape of the 2010s was one rich with the dialogue of progress. Though the battle for civil rights has been met with setbacks along the way, the voices and needs of society's most vulnerable people are succeeding in capturing the public eye. Activists have won many victories in seeking equal rights for people of all races, classes, religions, genders, and sexualities. Overwhelmingly, the most heated fights of the decade involved lesbian, gay, bisexual, and transgender (LGBT) people. Victories such as marriage equality and an expanding LGBT influence in politics and pop culture were met by conservative setbacks.

The rights of transgender people and the nature of their identities have particularly been the subject of significant debate, legislation, and discussion. Voices like Caitlyn Jenner, Janet Mock, Laura Jane Grace, and Chaz Bono have drawn a celebrity spotlight toward issues regarding gender identity. On the other hand, legislation that takes away rights from transgender people has been introduced in various American states. Acts that permit discrimination on the grounds of gender identity in the workplace, in restrooms, in housing, in education, and throughout other aspects of life have impacted lives and captivated public attention.

Transgender celebrities, such as teen television personality and activist Jazz Jennings, have helped bring trans rights into the spotlight.

With such an amplified spotlight shining on transgender people, it has become important for all people to be aware of what being transgender can look like and how to support those who may fall under the transgender umbrella. It's vital to help trans people feel accepted, find resources, and navigate the complexities of gender identity and gender expression.

A person's gender identity is their internal sense of their own gender. People tend to convey their gender identity through clothing, hairstyle, behavior, voice, and various other means of gender expression. A person's gender identity and gender expression do not necessarily have any relation to that person's sex. Sex is a classification based on the configuration of one's body. Gender, on the other hand, tends to be tied up in social and cultural norms. Most people have an internal, deeply felt sense of their own gender. A simple definition of a transgender person is somebody whose gender identity does not match the gender they were assigned at birth.

Sex and gender identity both impact people on a personal level and can affect how they're seen in society. Transgender people in one way or another break with expectations with regards to gender and sex. A marked incongruence between one's experienced gender and assigned gender, resulting in a strong desire and conviction to be the other gender is known

Theodore Xander Frey, of Cutler Bay, Florida, questioned his identity from a young age before eventually coming out as an agender male.

as gender dysphoria. Gender dysphoria is a psychiatric diagnosis that reflects the distress, discomfort, anxiety, and depression caused by a sense of disconnect or incongruence between someone's assigned gender and their gender identity.

Gender dysphoria is very personal and can be intensified by different life circumstances. It can be very disorienting, confusing, and hurtful for a person to be labeled by society in a way that doesn't reflect who they are. Figuring out what that feeling is, where it comes from, and how to solve it can be a stressful, complicated, but ultimately rewarding journey.

Gender expression and identity mean something to everyone, in all races and classes. Anyone, at any age, can experience gender dysphoria or identify as transgender. Not everyone who is transgender experiences gender dysphoria, and not everyone who experiences gender dysphoria is transgender. Some consider themselves gender questioning and enjoy exploring gender while others look at their transgender experience as simply a part of their history or a medical condition. Exploring gender and its many forms can be helpful for those with gender dysphoria while also providing a new form of self-expression for those without.

People who want to explore their gender identity or experience gender dysphoria will have several questions as they approach the process of expressing who they really are. What is gender? What does it mean to be transgender or cisgender? What is gender dysphoria, and who experiences it? How do their experiences vary? Exploring these issues is crucial for any person ready to begin pondering what gender might mean to them.

Understanding Gender Dysphoria

Understandings and experiences of gender difference have varied across times and cultures. Modern society typically sees gender as a binary—man and woman, male and female, boy and girl. That limited definition may include a person's body parts (their sex), the roles they're expected to adhere to, the ways they might express themselves, and sometimes even who a person can be attracted to (their sexuality). When someone says "gender," they might mean something resembling this definition. More open definitions, however, seek to define gender as an innate feeling, regardless of body parts and societal expectations.

What Is Gender?

Gender, sex, and sexuality are different things. When someone's identity, body, or expression opposes the idea that all people can be sorted

Brooke Guinan is a transgender firefighter and trans activist in New York City. In this photo, she is standing in front of Engine 312 in Astoria, Queens.

into a labeled box based on the configuration of their body at birth, it can create a lot of conflict. Those whose gender identity and expression align with the gender they were assigned at birth are considered cisgender. Those whose identity blurs the lines and rubs against the idea of a binary model are considered transgender. The prefixes of these words—*trans* and *cis*—mean "opposite" and "on this side of" respectively.

With this understanding, it's important to note that being transgender can mean a lot of different things. People who were assigned male or female at birth but don't identify that way have many ways to express themselves as something other than a boy or a girl. Imagine a color wheel. If what society typically defines as boys and girls are somewhere on that color wheel, there are hundreds of other genders on the same wheel. Not everyone fits into this model, but it can be a helpful guide to

Art student Jess Fajardo considered himself a tomboy growing up. As an adult, he sees his gender as fluid and is more comfortable presenting as male.

understanding what gender can look like.

This idea is sometimes referred to as a gender spectrum, much like the color spectrum that makes up visible light. In the color wheel model, there are areas on the color wheel where specific colors blur into each other and some things don't have a color at all. It's equally valid to say that someone can be a mix of different genders or identify as not having gender whatsoever. Therefore, being transgender can include people who are transitioning from one gender to another, people who express themselves as a certain gender some of the time, people who don't have a gender at all, and just about everyone else who does not fit easily into the binary model of gender.

Gender means something to everyone. Even those who

Gender Identities

Everyone has a gender identity! The most familiar are generally woman and man, though there are ways to subvert and avoid these categories. People can break down those identities into being feminine or masculine—so, someone can identity as feminine, or femme, without identifying as a woman, or as masc, without identifying as a man. In addition, not everyone aligns with just one identity. Being genderfluid means swinging between multiple genders, while being genderqueer and nonbinary are about identifying as a combination of genders or being outside of the scope of the traditional gender binary. There are also categories like demigender to express the idea that someone can occupy portions of gender space but not all—for example, a demigirl is someone who occupies the range of space between girl and nonbinary. Someone can also be agender, meaning they have no gender at all. There are also gender identities specific to individual cultures, such as third gender, which is common in India and other countries in that part of the world, and two-spirit, a respected Native American identity that means a person embodies the spiritual qualities of both women and men. Remember that, no matter what, everyone's identity is valid, and anyone can be any gender that they wish.

identify as cisgender have a gender identity, or an internal sense of gender. People express their gender identity through their behavior, clothing, hairstyle, voice, and body characteristics, all of which can be considered as part of their gender expression. For example, if a person who was assigned male at birth grows up to express and identify as a boy, that means they are a cisgender boy. Understandings and expressions of gender can change over time, so there have been many ways to express one's gender throughout various cultures.

How Gender Dysphoria Works

Gender can be fun to play with for some people while being challenging to navigate for others. Because gender is a form of self-expression, it can be exciting to subvert and express yourself in a way that's different from the norm. However, because gender is also associated with cultural expectations about peoples' bodies and their roles in society, someone's internal sense of who they are and how they express that to the world can be hard to safely explore. When someone feels confused or sad about the way gender is imposed on them; when they want very badly to be a different gender; or when they live in a culture that restricts certain kinds of gender expression, that can cause gender dysphoria. As of 2013, the American Psychiatric Association defines gender dysphoria as "a conflict between a person's physical or assigned gender and the gender with which he/she/ they identify" that can cause "significant distress and/ or problems functioning associated with this conflict."

Many different elements can contribute to gender dysphoria. A person's upbringing, their nationality, their class, their race, their ability status, and other factors all play a role. Feminist theorist and legal scholar Kimberlé Crenshaw coined the theory of intersectionality to address the way someone's gender and race must be considered together to understand the oppressions they might face and the lives they might lead. Intersectionality is important to take into account when discussing gender dysphoria. People are going to experience gender dysphoria differently depending on their cultures' expectations of gender and how they are treated by the people around them. In fact, a study released by the Williams Institute at the UCLA School of Law in October 2016, showed that transgender people in general are more racially and ethnically diverse than the US general population. The way that diverse group experiences gender dysphoria most certainly reflects their intersectional backgrounds as individuals.

Not all transgender people experience gender dysphoria, but it is a common thread among many members of the trans community. Per a survey taken in 2016 by the Williams Institute at the UCLA School of Law, there are estimated to be 1.4 million transgender people in the United States. Many transgender people are themselves working to confront their own gender

Kalil Gonzales-Cohen identifies as a genderqueer Jewish transman, while his wife, Karin, identifies as a bisexual Chicana high femme.

dysphoria and help others who experience it to find strategies to overcome it. The primary struggle for transgender people throughout the world is how to express their real selves and be respected as such by society at large. This sort of self-expression is vital for transgender people to live full and healthy lives. For many, living that healthy life starts with addressing the symptoms of their gender dysphoria through the process of transition—referring to the physical, mental, and social act of expressing a gender identity that does not match the one assigned to them at birth.

Gender Dysphoria as a Term

Since 1952, the *Diagnostic and Statistical Manual of Mental Disorders* (*DSM*) has provided psychiatrists and psychologists with a guide on how to diagnose and treat patients battling a multitude of mental health issues, gender dysphoria among them. The history of gender dysphoria within the *DSM* mirrors that of homosexuality. Originally gender dysphoria, like homosexuality, was treated by the *DSM* as a mental disorder, an illness that could be treated by various therapies and must be treated as an illness. In 1973, the *DSM* committee removed homosexuality from this categorization. In 2013, gender dysphoria received the same elevation.

Until the release of the *DSM-5* in 2013, gender dysphoria was listed as "gender identity disorder," with a diagnosis and definition that focused primarily on "strong and persistent cross-gender identification" and "persistent discomfort about one's assigned sex or a sense of inappropriateness in the gender role of that sex." While these are still major factors in some people's experience of gender dysphoria, the acute focus on incongruity ignored the larger impact gender dysphoria can have and made it more challenging for those who sought to transition from continuing treatment throughout their lives.

Since insurance companies and health care providers base their treatment coverage on manuals like the *DSM*, the American Psychiatric Association acknowledged that the definition of gender identity disorder "would jeopardize access to care." Thus, in the *DSM-5,* the term was changed and the definition was broadened. The Huffington Post pointed out that this change reflected the fact that "the drafters of the new *DSM*-5 wanted to emphasize the importance of distress about the incongruity." The change from "gender identity disorder" to "gender dysphoria" guarantees continued access to treatment throughout someone's transition and reduces the stigma attached to words like "disorder."

Confronting Gender Dysphoria

Gender dysphoria can cause significant damage to a person's well-being. It can lead to stress, cause rifts with a person's family and friends, and exacerbate existing mental and physical health issues. A transgender person interviewed for the National Center for Transgender Equality's 2015 U.S. Transgender Survey described their experiences, saying, "I had suffered from anxiety and depression as a direct result of gender dysphoria. This caused me to become more and more unable to function in society as time went on." Finding strategies to manage gender dysphoria can help to ease symptoms like anxiety and depression. Many transgender people credit such strategies and the process of transition in helping them heal and find a new lease on life.

It's valuable to note that there is not one determined set of strategies that will work for all transgender people. Thanks to intersectionality, it's clear that the needs and backgrounds of transgender people throughout the world are different, and the strategies that work for one person's gender dysphoria will not necessarily work for everyone. Even steps as common as coming out as one's true gender and transitioning to that gender through medical and social means are not the ultimate path for everyone with gender dysphoria. Not everyone will feel good or safe in pursuing such a path. It is vital to include and consider the needs

The transgender community is full of unique experiences. Hundreds of thousands of people successfully manage gender dysphoria and go on to lead happy, healthy lives.

of each individual when exploring how to treat and confront gender dysphoria symptoms.

The most important thing to remember is that confronting gender dysphoria is very possible. Hundreds of thousands of people around the world do it every single day. If gender dysphoria refers to the feeling of unease and disconnect with regard to a person's assigned gender, then gender euphoria is its opposite, with the goal of treatment being a sense of harmony between one's identified gender, body, and self-expression. The strategies one uses are going to vary based on one's cultural background and precise gender identity. Fortunately, for nearly every trans person working to solve their personal struggle with dysphoria, there is someone who has been through a similar battle before them. For most people, there is a reasonable path to attaining a sense of resonance between one's gender identity and one's body, presentation, and societal treatment.

Myths & FACTS

Myth: Transgender people are confused and just need to be "fixed" so that they are comfortable with the gender they were born as.

Fact: While gender dysphoria is a mental health issue and can be confronted in many ways, someone's gender identity is never invalid regardless of how they were assigned at birth. Those who identify as transgender often needed an incredible amount of courage, strength, and support to express their identity to the world. They know who they are and deserve acceptance.

Myth: Anyone with gender dysphoria is transgender, all transgender people hate their bodies, and all transgender people get surgery and take medications.

Fact: Gender dysphoria is a sense of disconnection or incongruence between someone's assigned gender and their gender identity that can cause distress, discomfort, anxiety, and depression. For some, solving that distress does involve medical care. For others, merely

(continued on the next page)

Myths & FACTS

(continued from the previous page)

adopting a new gender presentation can help, while some rely on therapy to help them feel more comfortable in their assigned gender. There is no single path to solving gender dysphoria that works for everyone, though there are strategies available for anyone.

Myth: All transgender people are gay.

Fact: Gender and sexuality are different. Cisgender and transgender people alike can express love for other people in several ways—they can be gay, straight, asexual, bisexual, and so on. Whom people love often has nothing to do with their gender. While transgender people may have preferences for certain bodies or personalities, having such preferences is universal, and transgender peoples' tastes vary as much as cisgender peoples' do.

CHAPTER TWO

Gender Presentation

Consider the ways that people express themselves to each other and how often that sort of expression might reflect their gender. Society dictates expectations for how people might behave based on their gender. These kinds of expression are usually sorted into two categories, masculine and feminine. The expectations shape how people present themselves at work, at school, and with friends and family. Subverting these kinds of expression and asserting one's identity can be challenging, but incredibly freeing and rewarding. For those managing gender dysphoria, adopting a gender presentation that works for them can be the best place to start.

Dysphoria and Presentation

If someone feels pressured, by societal expectations and relationships with people around them, to

This transgender high school student is looking for a new outfit at a store in Manhattan. Clothing is one of the primary means of gender presentation.

act or look a certain way according to their assigned gender, that can cause dysphoria even if the person doesn't fully recognize it. Dysphoria is rarely explicit; it's uncommon for someone to recognize at first that the distress they're experiencing is related to the way they present themselves. Often, dysphoria can come in the form of *wanting* to express oneself in a particular way without necessarily knowing why or being jealous that other people are free to express themselves in a way that one feels restricted from. It can be scary and overwhelming for a person to change the way they present themselves, and that sort of change can impact their relationships with others.

For some, matching gendered perceptions can be incredibly validating. It can be great for some women, for example, to have the person in the mirror reflect what society believes a woman should look like. But perceptions aren't the entirety of what gender is. Someone can be a woman who loves watching sports and action movies and hates wearing makeup and still be a woman, if that's who they feel that they are. Expressing identity is about expressing oneself authentically, without compromise.

Imagine a hypothetical person. They experience dysphoria because of the gender and sex that were assigned to them at birth. They don't like having to move about the world in a way that reflects the societal expectations attached to that gender. Resolving that

After Harvard University added desired pronoun fields to its registration forms in 2015, student Laila Smith noted their use of they/them pronouns on the forms.

conflict comes in several parts. For starters, they'll want to start expressing themselves in a way that reflects who they want to be, rather than in a way that reflects who society believes they should be. They'll need to find strategies that make that kind of expression easy, safe, and manageable in a world that might not welcome subversion of gendered norms. Whether this means a transgender person who wants to present as a gender opposing the one they were assigned or a cisgender person looking to escape rigid social expectations, gender presentation can help someone find a way to show the world who they believe themselves to be.

Expressing Oneself Differently

Changing one's gender presentation can take many forms. For some, it means changing the way they look, from clothing to hair and more. For others, it means changing the pronouns they use to refer to themselves and asking others to do the same. It can mean that someone chooses to go by a new name. Gender presentation can be a scary and daunting thing to change. It requires a lot of courage, a little creativity, and a supportive group of friends and family to get right. Supporting the gender that someone presents as is vital. That includes respecting their pronouns and honoring their choices and decisions. All of this is made so much easier through understanding, caring, and consideration.

Pronouns

In everyday life, people are usually referred to in shorthand by "he," "she," and other gendered pronouns. For many, adopting a new gender pronoun is an early step in transitioning from one gender to another. Just like "man" and "woman" aren't the only genders, "he/him" and "she/her" aren't the only pronouns that people go by. Many nonbinary people have adopted the use of "they/them" as a nongender pronoun that can be used in everyday conversation. Other gender-variant people have pursued new pronouns, including "xe/xyr," "ze/hir," and pronouns used in other languages such as the Swedish "hen." For those unacquainted with gender-variant pronouns, adopting new pronouns to refer to their friends or family can be daunting. Using guides like the one available on Pronoun Island (pronoun. is) not only make it easier to understand the usage of newer pronouns, but also allow people to share what pronouns they use in a simple and easy way. Support those with alternative pronouns in day-to-day life by asking people around you what pronouns they prefer and sharing your own chosen pronouns whenever you can.

It's vital to remember that while many people with gender dysphoria choose to incorporate changing their gender presentation into their transition, this isn't going to be the preferred path for everyone, nor is it the only way to manage gender dysphoria. For many, presenting as a gender that wasn't assigned to them at birth isn't feasible or safe. Cost, legal restrictions, familial situations, abusive relationships, cultural expectations, and many other factors can impede someone from presenting their gender the way that they want. Finding strategies to confront such obstacles and supporting people who do so is hugely important.

A person endeavoring to change their presented gender may need help adopting those techniques. For some, this can include binding (the act of using restrictive clothing to bind one's breasts and create a flat appearance) or tucking (which refers to hiding traditionally male-assigned genitalia using special undergarments and other tools). For others, this means learning how to use or abandoning the use of makeup, cutting or growing their hair, training their voice to be higher or lower, or collecting a new wardrobe. Some people choose to use medical interventions to make these acts of gender presentation easier. Gender presentation can take someone from wishing they looked a certain way to actually appearing that way.

An important part of expressing one's identity fully is finding a name that feels good. Deciding on a

Andii Viveros, a transgender activist, chooses to wear makeup as she gets ready to host the annual Sun Serve LGBTQA Colors of the Wind youth prom in Fort Lauderdale, Florida.

name that feels right is a powerful tool in affirming one's identity. Imagine how harmful it would be for someone to go about everyday life and never have their identity acknowledged. It's important to trust that people know who they are at any given moment and deserve to be recognized as such.

Stacy Lynn Kilpatrick of Denver, Colorado, waits at the courthouse for her final legal name change paperwork. Changing one's name can be a time-consuming process.

Challenges in Change

Names and pronouns can change over time but should always be respected by others. Many transgender people refer to the names given to them by their parents as their dead names. For those people, hearing their dead name can cause significant dysphoria and a lot of psychological pain. Thus, many choose not to share details of a person's assigned identity, no matter the context.

Changing Legal Name and Gender

The process of changing one's legal name and gender differs from country to country and even from state to state. In the United States, legal name and gender change is a divisive process that changes depending on where someone was born or lives. Most states have easy name change processes that everyone can access. Certain states allow people to change their gender rather easily with simple legal forms. Others require documentation from medical professionals or certain surgeries. Though making legal changes can help improve a transgender person's daily life, the validity of someone's gender does not hinge upon their legal status.

In addition to barriers like cost, certain states, such as Tennessee, don't have legal gender change options. It was not until April 2016 that Oregon became the first state to allow legal gender changes that reflect nonbinary identities. Many trans feminine and trans masculine nonbinary people choose to change their legal gender to one that is more reflective of their transition experience and their particular expression. For those who experience cost as a barrier, some states, including California and Oregon, offer name/gender change fee waivers. In addition, there are organizations, such as the Transgender Law Center, that will offer guides and even financial assistance for those looking to change their name and gender. Organizations like Mermaids UK and Trans Equality Canada seek to help those outside the United States.

For undocumented immigrants, migrant status can impact not only access to legal changes but to treatment options and supportive communities as well. For immigrants, class barriers compound with large delays surrounding document changes and the threat of abuse in their home countries. In the United States, immigrants have access to name and gender change options, thanks to changes made in 2012 to the US Citizenship and Immigration Services guidelines. Immigrants looking for assistance in their gender transition can find help through organizations like the Sylvia Rivera Law Project and the Transgender Law Center.

A lot of transgender people go to great lengths to ensure their gender identity and expression are acknowledged throughout their lives. They communicate their need for respect to others through actions like changing their name legally and working to have their name and gender recognized by family, friends, classmates, and colleagues. For some, this also means working with their schools or workplaces to use the correct restroom facility safely or wear a uniform more befitting of their gender identity.

People who attempt to change their name and gender can face opposition from peers, governments, and employers. There has been progress for some. For example, in December 2016, New York issued its first intersex birth certificate to Sara Kelly Keenan, acknowledging Sara's identity and status as neither male nor female. However, opposition and controversy has erupted over transgender peoples' right to assert their identities. Throughout 2015, Facebook came under pressure from transgender-allied organizations such as the Transgender Law Center to change its name policy, which had required users to use the name listed on their ID and left transgender users vulnerable to frivolous bans. Worse, laws that respect transgender identities can change according to political whims. For example, in January 2017, the website Nuvo reported that Indiana state representative Bruce Borders had filed House Bill 1361, "which would prohibit any change on a birth certificate and the permanent birth record of the gender of an individual," leaving transgender people born in Indiana at risk of never having their identities fully acknowledged by the law. It's important to help reduce such opposition and always acknowledge a

Demonstrators protested the enactment of North Carolina's HB2, a "bathroom bill" that restricted trans people from using public facilities matching their gender identities.

person's identity regardless of the legal challenges they may be facing.

Policies and politics may get in the way of a person's goals, but supportive communities and alternative means of gender presentation can help someone subvert such challenges. Some transgender people only present their identities in safe spaces, such as online communities or support groups. Some choose to live a stressful "double life," adopting their true identities where it's safe and wearing their assigned identities like a mask where it's not. Many transgender people are forced to dead name and misgender themselves in procedural settings just to get by. This can mean applying for jobs under a long-incorrect name or presenting themselves differently in government buildings. Finding ways to balance someone's actual identity and the unfortunate necessity of maintaining their previous self is crucial to ultimately achieving gender harmony.

Those who don't face as many risks and barriers will often choose to "come out," asserting their gender identity throughout all aspects of life. Many of these people aim to completely blend in as the gender they are presenting, without the risk of anyone seeing them as their assigned gender. In the transgender community, this is commonly called passing. While someone's gender doesn't hinge upon the opinions of other people, passing can be extremely validating for transgender people and others with gender dysphoria. Passing can also be important because it mitigates various risks that come with presenting as a gender that doesn't match the gender a person was assigned. Those risks include psychological damage, physical harm, and legal implications, all considered forms of transphobia.

Gender presentation is a massive part of confronting gender dysphoria and living as one's true gender. Expressing oneself with hairstyles, clothing, makeup, and other things are important to everyone and can be especially affirming to someone's gender identity. While passing as one's identified gender is not important to all transgender people, for many it can make a huge difference in their everyday life and health. Adopting a new name and pronoun can be challenging but helps someone navigate the world in a way that respects who they really are. Health care providers and supportive communities can help transgender people combat transphobia and present their gender identity more fully and more safely. Ultimately, gender presentation can help everyone express who they are, and there are many components to making sure proper gender presentation is possible for those seeking to transition.

CHAPTER THREE

Medical Care

Some people find medical therapies to be a critical step in furthering their transition and managing their gender dysphoria. Pursuing strategies such as hormone replacement therapies and gender affirmation surgeries can be very important for some transgender people. These techniques can change a person's body in ways that make them feel more comfortable and resonant with their sense of self. They can affirm someone's identity and help lessen the symptoms of dysphoria. Since culture's perceptions of gender are tied to certain traits of the body, then it only makes sense that some people aim for their bodies to match their own perceptions or the perceptions of others. There are many obstacles that can block someone's ease of access to medical treatment, but supportive medical professionals and communities can help pave the way.

Be aware that someone's body isn't the be-all, end-all of their gender identity. Nor will medical strategies work to ease everyone's gender dysphoria. However, for those whose experience of gender dysphoria is tied to certain physical traits, strategies that center around medical treatment can be a great way forward. In addition, even those who don't experience dysphoria, such as cisgender people, can benefit from some of these medical strategies.

Caring for All Bodies

The medical treatments employed to help confront dysphoria and allow people to have bodies that more accurately reflect social expectations of their gender identity have been standardized over time. The 2015 US Transgender Survey found that a clear majority of transgender respondents sought medical care as part of their transition, with 78 percent of respondents wanting to incorporate hormone therapy, 77 percent wanting mental health care, and 25 percent having undergone some form of transition-related surgery. Doctors throughout the world have been employing strategies like these to help transgender people since the early 1900s. The World Professional

Jenn Brewer, a young transgender man, received the appropriate treatment for his transition from Dr. David Klein in Fort Belvoir, Virginia.

Association for Transgender Health maintains that gender-affirming treatments "play an undisputed role in contributing toward favorable outcomes" and are proven to improve the lives of those with gender dysphoria. Medical care can be an important means of helping someone tackle gender dysphoria and be more comfortable in their own skin.

It has been said in the past that transgender people are "born in the wrong body." While this is generally considered inappropriate and doesn't reflect the experiences of everyone, it can be an accurate way for some people to articulate their experiences and their feelings. Many would prefer to have been born with different physical traits, some of which can be induced by rewiring the body to produce a kind of hormone that aligns with their gender identity and others can be introduced by means of various surgeries.

Intersex Bodies

It's important to remember that there are bodies with individual needs that won't adhere to the binary-oriented treatment that most transgender people receive. While many people think that all human bodies can be classified as male or female, this ignores bodies that vary from that rigid standard. First, many people who are assigned one sex at birth develop traits that are traditionally associated with the other. Second, there are many people whose bodies simply don't align with the binary system. Those people, whose genitalia or chromosomal makeup may differ from sexual norms, are considered intersex.

Many intersex people identify as somewhere under the transgender umbrella due to the way gender is imposed on them at birth. Throughout history, intersex people have been cast aside into other categories or have been assigned by doctors into one gender category or another based on their genitalia. Worse, some doctors will actively manipulate the bodies of intersex people at birth to make them look the binary sex they're being coercively categorized as. The experiences of intersex people can be sensitive, personal, and uniquely complex, and the treatment many of them receive at birth can cause heightened dysphoria later in life. The needs and bodies of intersex people must be considered when discussing medical treatment.

Hormone Replacement Therapy

Hormone replacement therapy (HRT) is a common means of addressing dysphoria about the body. It's the way that many begin the process of transitioning. When employed alongside strategies like changing gender presentation, it can help make the social and legal parts of transition easier. This sort of medical transition can be started at any stage in life. Its effects and the medications used will change from person to person. Often, the kind of treatment that works for someone is dependent on their age and assigned sex.

There are several ways to administer hormones as part of a transition. Generally, the treatment pursued hinges on a person's assigned sex and physical makeup. Bodies that are assigned female at birth typically produce estrogenic hormones in the estrone family of steroids, like estrogen, while bodies that are assigned male typically produce androgenic hormones and steroids, including testosterone.

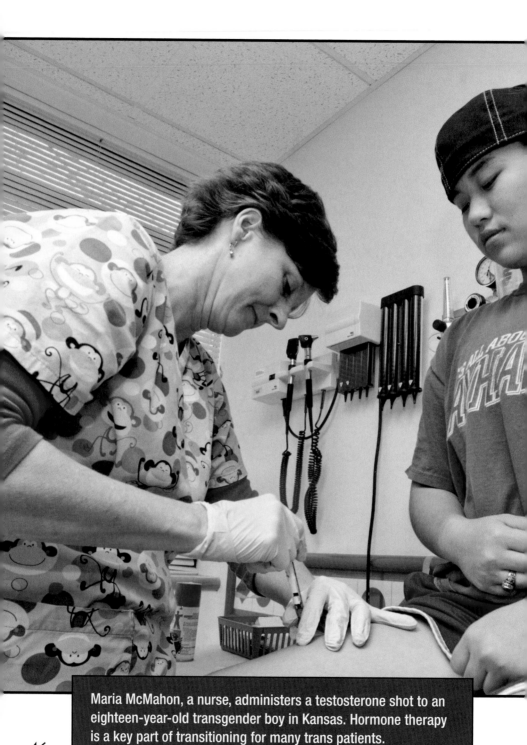

Maria McMahon, a nurse, administers a testosterone shot to an eighteen-year-old transgender boy in Kansas. Hormone therapy is a key part of transitioning for many trans patients.

For example, if someone assigned male at birth identifies as a girl, they will want to pursue treatment that makes their body more in line with the body of someone who would be assigned female at birth. In that case, treatment would involve medications (known as antiandrogens) that block the production of anabolic steroids, such as testosterone and the addition of estrogenic hormones, like estradiol and progesterone. These medications can be taken through external patches, gels, pills, and injections. Sometimes the way hormones are ingested and the amount given changes based on the trajectory of a person's transition.

To explore how this might play out, imagine someone who was assigned female at birth, identifies as nonbinary, and wants the world at large to perceive them as typically masculine.

Hormone therapy can help because, for that person, the application of testosterone can help end monthly periods, reduce the prominence of their breasts, and encourage the production of hair growth, in addition to naturally lowering the pitch of their voice. All of this can help the person move about the world in a way that's more reflective of their identity while making them more comfortable in their own skin.

Those beginning hormone replacement therapy at a younger age may require a different set of therapies than others. The body doesn't start producing sex hormones until puberty, which begins around age ten for those assigned female at birth and around age eleven for those assigned male. A kind of medication called a puberty blocker allows families "to hit a pause button," according to a PBS *Frontline* interview with Dr. Rob Garofolo, of the Lurie Children's Hospital. Puberty blockers can prevent and delay puberty, giving young people "the time and space to explore and settle on their gender identity" without having to worry about the hormones produced during puberty having permanent effects on their bodies.

Surgical Options

Hormone therapies can only do so much. While they can influence the development of breasts or body hair and impact mood and emotions, they often don't cause all of the changes a transgender person may desire. The gaps left by hormone therapy don't bother everyone, but for those who are looking for more, there are many surgical options available to continue the transition process. Unlike hormone replacement therapy, access to these surgeries can be limited by access to regional care and the occasional necessity of letters of support from other health care providers. In some places, such surgeries can be necessary for changing legal documentation as well. Surgery is not the end-all be-all of someone's gender, but it can be very affirming for many and necessary for legal change for some.

As with hormone replacement therapy, the surgeries someone chooses to undergo are usually determined by their assigned sex. For those who were assigned male at birth, the surgeries typically used include vaginoplasty, in which a doctor reshapes traditionally male genitalia like the penis and testicles into a vagina; orchiectomy, a surgery which removes a person's testicles; breast enhancement, which usually acts in addition to breast growth promoted by hormone therapy; facial feminization surgery, in which the face is augmented to have a more traditionally feminine appearance; and trachea shaving, which reduces the appearance of the Adam's apple on the neck and can heighten the pitch of one's voice. Those surgeries are usually accompanied by hair removal techniques such as laser or electrolysis, as hormones alone can't

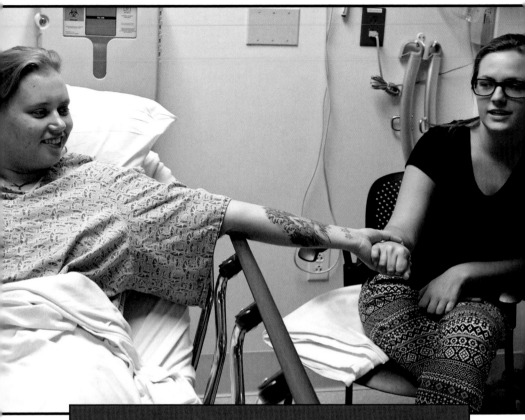

EJ Silverberg holds hands with his girlfriend before his mastectomy, a common surgery for trans men, at Beth Israel Deaconess Medical Center, in Boston, Massachusetts.

completely cease the growth of facial and body hair in most people. For those assigned female at birth, available surgeries include mastectomy, the removal of breasts in order to give the chest a flat appearance, and phalloplasty, which describes the construction of a penis from traditionally female genitalia. Testosterone is far more aggressive than estrogen, so trans masculine individuals and transgender men usually will not require surgeries focused on modifying their faces or their voices.

Bypassing Barriers to Care

Learning about this kind of care can be a tough journey for some. While most medical organizations endorse guidelines for transgender health care and many doctors will adhere to and support people based on those guidelines, many trans people do not get the medical care they need and deserve. The 2015 US Transgender Survey reported that 55 percent of those who sought coverage for transition-related surgeries were denied, that 25 percent of those who sought hormone coverage were denied, that 33 percent of those who saw a doctor in the previous year had negative experiences related to their gender identity, and that 56 percent of respondents overall had difficulty seeing a doctor at all due to fear of mistreatment or barriers regarding cost.

Some doctors will go as far as getting in the way of care. Their negative attitudes toward transgender people and their belief that cisgender identities are more valid informs their perspective and drives them to block transgender individuals from treatment or perform conversion therapies that seek to "cure" them into being cisgender. As of 2017, many places throughout the United States and elsewhere have sought to ban such therapies, which may target cisgender gays and lesbians as well as transgender people. Those with gender dysphoria should never have to educate their doctors, though the unfortunate truth is that not all people are going to have access to compassionate coverage and must rely on the help of their communities to get the health care and therapy they need.

Organizations such as the World Professional Association for Transgender Health (WPATH) and University of California, San Francisco's Center of Excellence for Transgender Health maintain guidelines for treatment such as WPATH's highly regarded Standards of Care, which informs several insurance companies in the United States. Support groups, such as TRANS:THRIVE in San Francisco, and online communities, such as MyTransHealth, dedicate themselves to helping transgender people find resources and many transgender people report having heard about treatment options by word of mouth. LGBT law organizations like Lambda Legal sometimes maintain resources concerning equal access to health care. Many cities and schools run LGBT and gay/straight alliance organizations that can help people find resources. Even finding transgender communities on social networks like Facebook, Twitter, and Tumblr can be hugely influential for someone who doesn't have access to a supportive health care provider.

These communities serve to help educate, in addition to finding resources to counter financial and legal barriers. Not everyone has the insurance coverage, financial means, or legal status to access care. Some organizations, such as San Francisco's Lyon Martin Health Services, provide free or low-cost care to transgender people regardless of their insurance status. Resources like Canada's Trans-Health online magazine have compiled clinics like this in several regions worldwide. Further, online communities like Reddit's trans*health provide lists of resources for transgender people and a forum for people to discuss their health care needs. Legal barriers to care can include state health care policies and age requirements. The legal age of consent for any kind of medical care, including transition-related care, can vary from place to place, and minors often require parental or guardian consent unless they are emancipated from their parents or such care is ordered by a court. Most state Medicaid programs, for example, do not cover transition-related health care, though patients in states such as California, Oregon, Minnesota, and Massachusetts have found success in getting this coverage. The same resources

Zakia McKensey, an outreach specialist, speaks with a transgender woman about her prescriptions at the Fan Free Clinic in Richmond, Virginia.

that provide health care advice will often have advice regarding legal barriers, too.

Having access to care can help someone with gender dysphoria tremendously in achieving wellness. Therefore, it's important to understand the barriers to finding care. While specific medical procedures and treatments might not be right for every transgender person, knowing about what medical options exist and what communities can provide access to them is essential.

CHAPTER FOUR

Combating Transphobia and Cissexism

Gender dysphoria is a complicated thing to handle. It requires a lot of bravery and strength to confront the symptoms of dysphoria and begin the process of transition. Those who identify as transgender or deal with gender dysphoria in their daily lives know the kind of personal hardship dysphoria and transition can cause. Things shouldn't be that way, but unfortunately, people outside of the traditional gender binary face a set of biases and oppressions along their paths to wellness and self-expression. Transphobia and cissexism impact transgender people throughout life, particularly at home, at school, at work, in medical care, and in public life.

What Is Transphobia?

Transphobia refers to language and behavior that seeks to belittle, diminish, erase, or harm transgender people. This can include everything from laws that block transgender people from using public facilities to violence enacted against transgender people throughout the world. Cissexism is the primary driver of transphobia. It's the idea that cisgender people—their identities, their bodies, their experiences—are somehow more valid, valuable, or important than transgender people.

What does cissexism look like? How does transphobia harm transgender people? Cissexism is when a politician writes a bill proposing that bathrooms be assigned by "chromosomes at birth," or the "sex assigned on a person's birth certificate." It's when an airport security checkpoint features a body scanner with two buttons, a pink button and a blue button, subjecting anyone whose bodies don't align with these vague categories to invasive pat downs and body searches. Ideas and actions like these create a rigid system in which gender and sex are somehow intrinsically linked and can never be modified.

Risks are introduced when a transgender person is perceived as visibly trans, or clocked; when they're referred to by their assigned gender and the wrong pronoun, or misgendered; and when others use the name they were given at birth, or dead named. These all fall under the umbrella of microaggressions. The term was initially coined by Harvard professor Chester M. Pierce to refer to dismissive insults used specifically

Gendered restrooms can cause transgender people a unique amount of stress, especially as laws determining access can vary state by state.

by nonblack Americans toward black Americans, and is now used to describe that kind of abuse toward any minority group. Unlike more blatant forms of transphobia, microaggressions can be subtle and even unintentional. Nevertheless, microaggressions betray an ingrained cissexism that the person committing them might not even be aware of. Telling someone that they are "pretty for a trans woman," asking personal questions about a person's medical, romantic, or sexual history, or offering unsolicited advice about how to look more "like a man" are all examples of transphobic microaggresions.

In addition to amplifying their dysphoria, transphobia can expose gender-variant individuals to further hardships. The 2015 US Transgender Survey reported high rates of harassment, economic hardship, employment instability, and homelessness in the trans population, all stemming from transphobia. Nearly half of respondents, for example, reported having been verbally harassed in the past year. As of 2016, due to increasing legal instability and attacks on transgender people specifically in the United States, transphobia has also led to the barring of transgender people from access to public restroom facilities and health care coverage. One in ten respondents to the 2015 US Transgender Survey reported having been denied access to a restroom in the prior year, with many more reporting having to avoid using a public restroom or seeking health care due to fear of mistreatment.

Transmisogyny and Racism

While all transgender people suffer the risks of transphobia and cissexism, it's important to consider intersectionality when looking at the kind of risks that people may encounter in their daily lives. In modern society, women and members of racial and ethnic minorities are often the most vulnerable. They face various forms of bigotry, including misogyny, directed toward women; racism, directed toward black people, Asian people, people of Hispanic descent, and other people of color; and ethnic or religious discrimination, directed toward Muslims, Jews, Hindus, and other groups.

The impact of these kinds of discrimination extends to transgender people as well. According to the National Coalition of Anti-Violence Program, as of 2014, transgender people who were black were 1.6 times more likely to suffer physical violence than those who were not. Trans people of Hispanic descent were more than twice as likely to experience threats and intimidation. The Human Rights Campaign expanded upon this, saying that transgender women of color were uniquely vulnerable to violence, harassment, and other discrimination.

Many trans people are also specifically impacted by transmisogyny, abuse and microaggressions directed specifically at transgender women and trans feminine people who were assigned male at birth. Transmisogyny and racism leave transgender women of color more at risk than any other minority group. In addition, transmisogyny drives a significant amount of institutional transphobia, as most "bathroom bills" are promoted on the basis of keeping "men out of women's restrooms," specifically implicating transgender women as inherently dangerous. Many groups work to protect those affected by these unique forms of transphobia and raise awareness about their harmful effects. Understanding how transmisogyny and racism work together is vital to mitigating risk and creating equality for all.

Everyone's individual story with transphobia is different. According to the 2015 US Transgender Survey, transgender people rely on a variety of sources of support. Of those who reported their experiences with coming out, 60 percent found support from their families, 68 percent found support from their coworkers, and 56 percent found support from their friends. This kind of support is hugely beneficial, with

Transgender teens, like Adam Beaty, are better off when they receive support from their parents. Adam's mother, Liza, has been supportive of her son.

family support playing a key role in maintaining economic stability, access to health care, avoiding homelessness, and staving off psychological distress, including thoughts of suicide. While many trans people find support, the path to acceptance, particularly for young people, isn't always easy.

At Home

It is not uncommon for families to be hostile or abusive to transgender family members or to refuse or be resistant to recognizing their gender, pronouns, or name. An upsetting 10 percent of respondents to the US Transgender Survey reported a family member being violent toward them, and 8 percent reported being kicked out of their homes and pushed into homelessness. Some families will even push young people into harmful conversion therapies and force them to hide their identities even after coming out.

This kind of abuse can occur in romantic relationships as well. *Nobody* has to stay in an abusive relationship, for any reason. Many people, particularly those made more vulnerable by intersectional oppression, feel pressured to do so for several reasons, not the least of which include avoiding homelessness and attaining financial security. Know that there are organizations that can help vulnerable lesbian, gay, bisexual, transgender, and other queer people escape abusive situations. The National Domestic Violence Hotline acts as an always-available resource for those looking for help in abusive family, roommate, or romantic situations, and it maintains a list of resources specifically catering to LGBT people.

School and Work

Outside of the home, transgender people can face difficulty in school and at work. Many transgender students and workers face transphobia and cissexism from their classmates, coworkers, teachers, managers, and school leadership. In school, cissexism maintains rigid binary dress codes, gendered bathrooms, locker rooms, and sports teams, while supporting a curriculum that ignores the existence of transgender people. Transphobia can leave transgender students struggling to have their identities recognized by school

Homelessness

Being pushed out of one's home is an unfortunate and scary experience for many transgender youth. For some, leaving home and living on the streets is a survival tactic—the streets become their home. Navigating homeless shelters can be extremely challenging, with many transgender people reporting harassment in shelters or avoiding shelters altogether due to fear of mistreatment. Laws that restrict people from finding shelter in public spaces can cause transgender youth a significant amount of harm. For many homeless trans youth, finding community is their only means of survival, relying on the goodness of their peers and support agencies to get by.

If you or someone you know is suffering homelessness and needs queer- and youth-specific resources, there is help. The National Center for Transgender Equality maintains a database of rights regarding housing, homelessness, and access to shelters. They can also connect you with local organizations and support hotlines that can connect you with a housing and homelessness expert in your area.

administration and fighting for recognition on their own.

Finding support from individual classmates, teachers, librarians, and administrators can be a big step forward for many. As legal battles continued throughout 2016 and 2017 over what facilities and protections were available for transgender students, organizations like the Transgender Law Center and Lambda Legal published guides that help transgender students and their allied educators advocate for change. Classmates came together to support their peers, through protest and using organizations like GLSEN (Gay, Lesbian and Straight Education Network) and GSA Network (Genders & Sexualities Alliances) to collect resources for themselves and educators alike. While it can be a struggle, it's more than possible to foster positivity, celebrate queer history, and found campus organizations dedicated to educating and protecting lesbian,

Finding a supportive group of peers at school can be an incredibly validating experience for many gender-variant students.

gay, bisexual, transgender, and other queer students.

At work, transgender people of all ages face similar issues. Many face harassment from managers, coworkers, customers, and clients. According to the National Center for Transgender Equality, more than one in four transgender people have lost their jobs because of transphobia, while more than 75 percent have experienced other discrimination in the workplace. At work, trans people may contend with bathroom use, gendered uniforms, potential violence, and exclusive insurance policies. They can end up fighting even to get hired, risking potential privacy violations, and confronting laws that don't leave them protected from employment discrimination.

Living Life Safely

Many transgender and gender non-conforming people experience harassment—and sometimes even violence—just walking down the

Alexia Daskalakis, a transgender woman, was fired from her job as she began her transition. Unfortunately, many trans people face discrimination in the workplace.

street. Changing legal documentation can be time consuming and expensive. But without documentation, trans people are often exposed to a lack of legal protections and discrimination at the hands of police. Transgender women and transgender people of color are at an increased risk due to transmisogyny and racism. Transgender immigrants are also impacted by oppression and discrimination from Border Patrol agents and misplaced in gendered detention centers, where they can be mistreated and denied care.

Many transgender people confront these risks every single day. They do it by finding organizations that can help, relying on their bravery, acting on their truths, and asserting their identities. Keeping oneself safe can mean resorting to tough strategies. It can mean taking self-defense classes, carrying pepper spray and other self-defense tools, and traveling in packs. It can mean relying on resources like Refuge Restrooms to find safe facilities. All over the world, allies for transgender people fight for the people they care about, too. Understanding the risks of transphobia and knowing how to rely on the community to confront it is essential for coping with gender dysphoria.

10 Great Questions to Ask a School Administrator

1. Does our school have a policy regarding transgender students?

2. Would a transgender student at this school have access to restrooms, locker rooms, sports teams, activities, or uniforms that are congruent with their gender identity and expression?

3. Do you know someone transgender in life outside school?

4. Does our school have an LGBT club such as a gay-straight alliance?

5. If someone were to come out as transgender at our school, would school leadership tell their family?

6. Who would a transgender student talk to if they want to transition safely in school?

7. Does our library have any books on LGBT issues?

8. What does our school do to prevent bullying toward LGBT students?

9. Can our school participate in LGBT community events like Pride Day and Transgender Day of Remembrance?

10. Can we talk about transgender issues in class?

CHAPTER FIVE

Dysphoria and Mental Health

Gender dysphoria isn't the rift between someone's assigned gender and their identity, but the immense distress that this rift can cause. That distress can wreak havoc on a person if not kept in check. This means that people with gender dysphoria suffer unique risks when it comes to their mental health care. Gender dysphoria and transphobia work together to fuel depression and anxiety while exacerbating other mental health issues. Part of finding wellness and overcoming gender dysphoria is working to become whole again after a potential lifetime of confusion, disconnection, and fear.

A Bridge to Understanding

Note that this section will discuss suicide and self-harm.

It's hard to overstate the importance of mental health care when talking about gender

High school student Scott Morrison, of Portland, Oregon, says that transitioning and working with a counselor vastly improved his mental health.

dysphoria. When the news and various studies talk about transgender people, discussion of suicide risk and depression is quickly attached. It's important to make one thing clear: there are people within the transgender community who are scared, vulnerable, and think about and sometimes do things that can put their lives in danger. It can be a hard thing to talk about, but being open and honest about negative feelings and thoughts is an incredibly important first step toward getting the help needed to cope with these challenges and begin the healing process.

When You Need Help

If you or someone you know is considering suicide or is at immediate risk of violence or abuse, know that there is help. You are not alone. Know that it can help tremendously to talk to someone and that your feelings are completely valid. It's okay to be scared. It's okay to be upset. Write it down if you can, open Notes on your phone and type out how you're feeling, or even talk to your pet about it. Be honest about how you're feeling. It's important to get those feelings out.

Don't wait, talk to someone. Call someone you trust, reach out to someone online or a friend in the community, or call a hotline. There are many twenty-four-hour hotlines in the United States and abroad that can help discuss issues pertaining to trans youth. Try the Trans Lifeline (US: 877-565-8860, CAN: 877-330-6366), the Trevor Project (US: 866-488-7386, online chat open worldwide), or the National Suicide Prevention Hotline (US: 800-273-8255). If it's someone you know who is considering suicide, *stay with them*. Talk to them online or in person as much as you can. Offer to go to their house if you can, and if they're at real risk, consider going even if they say no. Encourage them to contact a mental health professional; offer to go with them.

This crisis is temporary. Understand that transgender people pushed into this situation aren't doing it on purpose and can often be harmed by methods of seeking help. Police can often be transphobic and elevate a situation, especially when considering people of color. Call the police only if the situation absolutely calls for it. They can then do a wellness check to make sure the person's OK and connect them with resources if they're not—otherwise, work with a crisis line or a medical-specific hotline first.

No matter what, remember to breathe. Remember that you or your friend will get through this. Take it slowly and take care of yourself. As the crisis dies down, put on some music, have a snack, play a video game, or watch reruns of your favorite show. Do whatever you can to calm the situation down. You can get through this and this will pass.

Ensuring transgender people are truly healthy starts by building a bridge from fear to openness when it comes to mental health issues. It is more than just a question of statistics. They exist—the 2015 US Transgender Survey says 40 percent of transgender people have attempted suicide in their lifetimes, nearly nine times the attempted suicide rate in the general US population. But even *one* person considering, attempting, or committing suicide is too many and should be enough to make this issue important and worth discussing. Outside of suicide, some transgender people will self-harm, through drug and alcohol abuse or through self-mutilation. Remember that people affected by thoughts of suicide or engaging in self-harm behavior need patience, understanding, and care. Transition and confronting gender dysphoria head-on can help strengthen self-acceptance in order to pull away from that darkness.

Many transgender people, their friends, their colleagues, and their families can tell stories of people that they've lost and relay experiences concerning self-harm. Transgender people often fight from the margins to get help managing their gender dysphoria, and sometimes, the fight becomes overwhelming. The first step is knowing how to get help. The second is taking that knowledge and using it to help someone else. Trans people and their allies fight hard to get better, every single day, at talking to each other about depression and the risk of suicide and how to help connect those who are struggling with the resources they need.

Talking about the risk of suicide is the hardest part of confronting gender dysphoria, but it's not the only mental health issue that dysphoria can cause. Being more aware of the mental health challenges that come with dysphoria can improve peoples' lives—and even save lives.

Eli, a trans teen in Fort Lauderdale, Florida, found his struggles with identity to be painful, experiencing heavy dysphoria due to his body.

Neurodivergent Paths

Dealing with dysphoria—and transphobia—can be incredibly hard and can inform every aspect of a person's life, including mental health. That means potentially causing and exacerbating various mental health conditions, including anxiety, depression, and posttraumatic stress disorder (PTSD). It also means that people who were born neurodivergent, like those with bipolar disorder and those on the autism spectrum, will have interactions with dysphoria and being transgender that look different from the experiences of neurotypical people.

Experiencing neurodivergence does not define a person, nor does it make them or their experiences any less valuable. People who experience depression, who are autistic, or who are neurodivergent in any of countless other ways still have the right and ability to feel happy, safe, nourished, and fulfilled. In the trans community, people experiencing various degrees of mental health issues are common, with only 10 percent of respondents to the 2015 US Transgender Survey reporting that psychological distress had not interfered with their life in any way. Even the most well-adjusted transgender person will struggle due to societal challenges, let alone if one has preexisting mental health issues, as well. That's why talking about mental health care and managing mental health issues are so important when addressing gender dysphoria; these experiences add to the richness of the transgender story.

Many transgender people will attest to transition helping them confront these issues. A respondent to the 2015 US Transgender Survey told this story

A Note on Gatekeeping

Medical institutions sometimes deny trans-specific health care, such as HRT, to individuals with certain forms of neurodivergence, such as schizophrenia. No one should be denied access to care. In the past, dysphoria and being transgender were defined as "mental illnesses," which was used as a tactic to justify denying the agency of transgender people. Many trans people who are hospitalized for suicidal ideation are at risk of losing access to their health care and hormones. These struggles are entirely unfair and put people at unnecessary risk. Working with community agencies such as MyTransHealth and the Transgender Law Center can help people find solutions for care in their area and get advice on how to overcome institutional gatekeeping.

well, saying, "I spent decades torturing myself into depression because I was certain that coming out would destroy my life. I did everything I could to get my transness to go away but it left me psychologically weak, and on the verge of suicide." For people like this, embracing who they are is a crucial part of healing. The

USTS's data shows that the rate of psychological distress experienced by transgender people falls tremendously as time passes from the beginnings of their transitions.

Transition alone won't solve mental health issues for everyone. In the case of those born neurodivergent, mental health is a pervasive theme throughout their lives. Transphobia, and the violence and instability that come with it, can exacerbate mental health issues no matter how long someone has been in transition. Pursuing regular mental health care is the way forward for many and can become a vital part of someone's transition.

Resources for Care and Crisis

Self-care means seeking out techniques for healing and crisis management that can be done on the fly at home, at school, and everywhere else. Self-care can be vital for managing symptoms of stress and anxiety, such as panic attacks. Relaxation techniques such as deep breathing, meditation, and yoga can make a big difference, In addition, techniques like "stimming" or self-stimulatory behavior can be essential for those born with disorders like autism, bipolar, and schizophrenia. Community websites like the Trevor Project provide ideas for self-care. There are several self-care inventory apps—including the University of the West of England, Bristol's, SAM—that can help manage anxiety. Most advise starting with simply acknowledging feelings. Self-care can be as broad as seeking out a mental health care professional and as small as taking a shower. Small, gratifying things, every single day, can make a huge difference. Listening to music, exercise, diet, sleep, wearing favorite clothes, reading, playing games, hanging out with friends—in times of crisis, even small moments of positivity turn a lot of

Apps like Self-Help for Anxiety Management and Booster Buddy along with a plethora of ways to talk to friends can make the internet and smartphones valuable mental health tools.

effort into emotional reward.

Therapists, psychologists, and psychiatrists can be helpful, though not all providers understand transgender experiences. Finding trans-affirming mental health care can be difficult and scary, but ultimately very rewarding. Sites like MyTransHealth help people throughout the United States find all kinds of trans-affirming medical care, including mental health care. Many schools offer on-campus mental health professionals who may be able to provide access to queer-friendly care. Local support groups will often have access to resources as well, with some queer centers going as far as offering drop-in counseling.

The most important thing to remember is everyone deserves a happy and healthy life. The path to wellness is going to look different for everyone. Sometimes, things get tough, and having self-care techniques and others resources at the ready is the best place to start. Learn how to talk about mental health issues and seek out local resources when possible. Transgender people deserve love and care, and there are many mental health providers who feel the same way.

Connection, Communities, and Relationships

The transgender community is rich and full, with people of all creeds, colors, and religions, from all corners of the globe. It's a diverse, friendly, and welcoming community, with a broad spectrum of perspectives, voices, and experiences to help guide newcomers and inspire resilience. The community's history is rich in cultural tradition and historic resistance. Trans people are dedicated to helping each other, and finding friends, family, and relationships within and outside of the queer umbrella can be immensely helpful for people facing gender dysphoria.

A History of Resilience

The transgender community is one that fights for itself. Many of the groups and foundations that work to further the cause of transgender welfare were founded by people under the transgender umbrella. In addition, transgender people have long been at the forefront of the fight for rights not just for those who are trans, but also for all queer-aligned people. Over time, growing acceptance, visibility, and access to technology has made the struggle for trans rights easier and provided new access to resources all over the globe.

One of the biggest misconceptions about transgender people is that being trans, and experiencing gender dysphoria, is a modern phenomenon. Cultural history shows that isn't true. While Western cultures have had a longstanding binary gender system, many other cultures allowed space for gender exploration before colonization and capitalism made that harder. In Native American traditions, for example, a two-spirit person is someone who embodies the spiritual presence of both men and women. Two-spirit people are incredibly valued in Native American cultural traditions, providing aid during childbirth and a vital place in many rituals and prayers. In another example, fa'afafine are a gender-variant group in the Samoan tradition who choose to embody masculine and feminine gender traits and perform traditionally

We'wha, a Zuni Native American from New Mexico, was an lhamana, (now known as mixed-gender or two-spirit), a male-assigned person who wears the clothing and fills the societal function traditional to Zuni women.

feminine duties in the home. The BBC reports that up to 5 percent of people in Samoa identify as fa'afafine.

Learning about these histories can be challenging, as the forces of cissexism fight to delegitimize the identities of transgender people. Even though gender nonconforming people have existed for generations, institutional information about trans experience is limited. The information that does circulate does so thanks to intracommunity efforts. Transgender people and their allies rely on each other to spread knowledge and inspire change.

Connecting with Others

The experience of gender dysphoria is deeply personal and can be very isolating, but no one is alone in their struggle. There are millions of transgender people throughout the world who have experienced the same feelings. Trans people can often feel isolated in their struggle, some in their desire to wake up in another body, others in their feeling of being lost in a maze of social expectations. Connecting with people who share the experience of being transgender or having dysphoria can be incredibly fulfilling. It can also help those looking to understand the condition of gender dysphoria find answers and allies in their journey of knowledge.

Marching with Pride

On June 28, 1969, patrons of the Stonewall Inn in New York City, raided by police, fought for their lives against arrest, public shaming, and institutional abuse. The Stonewall Inn was a congregating place for LGBT people throughout New York, whose identities were shoved to the absolute margins of society. Few establishments allowed gays, lesbians, and gender nonconforming people to congregate, and those that did were at risk of closure and loss of liquor licenses. Raids like this were routine, and often ended in torment, but on this night, they fought back. Patrons, led by trans women of color including Marsha P. Johnson and Sylvia Rivera, began throwing bricks at protesters and rallying patrons and passersby to protect the rights of the city's most marginalized people.

Back then, it was much harder to be queer, and many people like Johnson and Rivera identified as drag queens and survived on sex work. This was the case for many transgender women in particular— their identities were extremely misunderstood and heavily marginalized, much more so than in the present. Their heroic actions that night, along with the rest of the patrons at the Stonewall, sparked a

(continued on the next page)

(continued from the previous page)

movement that would give them, and all other LGBT people, more rights than ever before.

A year later, LGBT people celebrated the events at Stonewall by marching on Christopher Street Liberation Day, spurring other queer people to march in cities around the nation. That movement has ballooned into the Pride festivities that now happen all over the world every summer. Marsha P. Johnson and Sylvia Rivera continued to fight, founding groups to help homeless drag queens and transgender women of color and telling their stories to anyone who would listen.

Transgender people and their allies have access to more communities than ever before. In addition to Pride parades, the LGBT movement has spurred the existence of queer community centers in schools and cities around the globe. National organizations, like the Human Rights Campaign and the National Center for Transgender Equality, dedicate themselves to providing resources and institutional advocacy for trans and queer people. Groups like the Transgender Law Center, Lambda Legal, and the American Civil Liberties Union work tirelessly to defend transgender people in court.

This crowd of activists waved pink, blue, and white Trans Pride flags as they protested in North Carolina in support of transgender rights.

Outside of national organizations, transgender people are banding together in places around the United States and throughout the world. Many cities have trans lady picnics, trans support groups, and youth-specific groups, like TRANS:THRIVE at API Wellness San Francisco. Organizations like PFLAG seek to rally and educate families of queer people together. There are hundreds of opportunities to find community. There

Some camps are specifically aimed at trans youth. Here Tyler Sanchez, Chris Redick, and Nicole Maines paint the banner for a talent show at a transgender youth camp in Connecticut.

are hackathons, such as Trans*H4CK; queer camps, such as the University of California's yearly T-Camp; magazines, periodicals, such as Duke University's *Transgender Studies Quarterly*; game conventions, such as the Queerness in Games Conference and GaymerX; and even museums, such as the Museum of Trans History and Art, all dedicated to exposing trans exceptionalism and providing community and healing. Many of these resources can be found by word of mouth and in local magazines and, of course, many can be found online, too.

There are also many celebrations of trans identity, history, and resilience that happen worldwide every single year. Pride parades are the largest expression of this. Along with Pride, events like Transgender Awareness Month, which happens every November, seek to give transgender people and their allies a platform from which to talk about their needs. Transgender Day of Visibility, founded by activist Rachel Crandall in 2009, occurs each year on March 31 to celebrate trans people and raise awareness. Transgender Day of

Remembrance, on November 20, is an international day of action that has honored the lives of trans people lost to suicide and violence since 1999.

Social Media and Digital Connections

Social media can be an important tool for finding resources and friends for trans youth, especially those

Shannon Axe, a trans teenager in Lafayette, Colorado, monitors her YouTube channel and Instagram account, where she boasts thousands of followers.

outside of urban areas. Trans communities on Reddit, Tumblr, Twitter, and Facebook can be a safe way to make connections and seek information. Searching for tags concerning gender dysphoria and being transgender can be a great way to start. In exploring online resources, self-care is advised, as there can be harassment in online spaces and not everything read online should be trusted. Talking to community members in real life and seeking printed, published resources is a good way to find communities that are safe and trustworthy.

Love and Relationships

For many, finding a loving partner or partners, and sharing closeness with someone is really important and very special. Transgender people, like their cisgender counterparts, can express their sexuality in several ways. Gender identity doesn't necessarily impact sexuality and not all people are interested in seeking sexual relationships. Transgender people can be gay, straight, bisexual, asexual, demisexual, demiromantic, and anything in between. They fall in love and are loved by other trans people and cis people alike. Some trans people choose to date people of trans experience for safety and comfort reasons, while others find it validating to date cisgender people.

Isaac Barnett and his prom date Jasen, both trans, get ready for their prom in Kansas City, Missouri. Isaac and Jasen found friends and teachers more supportive then they had expected.

Safe relationship practices are as important for transgender people as they are for anyone else, if not more so due to increased rates of relationship abuse, HIV, and other sexually transmitted diseases in the trans population. Remember that no one deserves to be in a harmful relationship and that there are resources like the National Domestic Abuse Hotline that can help. As for everyone, it's important to practice safe sex by using condoms and birth control to avoid the transmission of disease and avert unintended pregnancy. While hormones have an impact on the ability for some transgender people to procreate, it's still wise to practice safe sex always and regularly talk to a doctor about sexual activity and STD testing.

Looking Forward

Dysphoria takes many forms but can provoke a deep feeling of alienation. The process of coping, then, means finding connections with others in the journey of discovering ourselves. As long as there have been people, there have been those who have lived outside of binary or normative understandings of gender, experienced dysphoria, and lived transgender and "other-gender" lives. There have always been strategies and tools to connect with and express one's internal self. Accessing those tools is now easier than ever before. There is a long shared history of trans resistance and trans culture. All people are valid, unique beings, with individual experiences, genders, and perspectives, coming to terms with their beautiful selves.

Glossary

binding The act of using restrictive clothing to bind ones breasts and create a flat appearance.

cisgender Referring to those whose gender identity and expression align with the gender they were assigned at birth.

cissexism The belief or assumption that cisgender people are better or more normal than transgender people.

femme Someone who identifies with and utilizes social traits that are traditionally associated with women and girls.

gender euphoria A sense of harmony between one's identified gender, body, social treatment, and self-expression.

gender expression The ways in which a person expresses their gender identity, including hairstyle, clothing, makeup, voice, mannerisms, and so forth.

gender identity Someone's internal sense of gender with regard to their self-image and ideal body and expression.

gender spectrum A model of gender identities that some consider outdated designed to reflect the idea that there are many gender identities outside of and in between man and woman.

gender-variant Experiencing gender on a way that falls outside of the male-female boundary.

intersectionality The way a person's gender, class, and race must be considered together in order to understand the oppressions they might face and the lives they might lead.

intersex Referring to people who possess any variation of genitalia or chromosomal makeup that does not fit the traditional binary of male and female.

masc Someone who identifies with and utilizes social traits that are traditionally associated with men and boys.

microaggression A casual insult to or dismissal of a member of a socially disadvantaged group. It lays bare prejudices that perpetrators may not know they have.

neurodivergent Describing people with conditions such as depression, anxiety, autism, and schizophrenia, whose neurocognitive functioning differs from the dominant social standards that are considered "normal."

nonbinary Referring to somebody who identifies as outside of the scope of the traditional gender binary. It can include genderqueer, genderfluid, demigender, and agender individuals.

passing In the trans community, this refers to the act of someone blending in as the gender they are presenting as, without the risk of anyone seeing them as their assigned gender.

stimming Repetitive movements, actions, or sounds that people use to calm or stimulate themselves.

transgender Referring to those whose gender identity and expression do not align with the gender they were assigned at birth.

transition The physical, mental, and social act of expressing a gender identity that does not match the one assigned at birth

transphobia Discrimination against transgender people.

tucking The act of hiding traditionally male-assigned genitalia using special undergarments and other tools.

Egale Canada

185 Carlton Street

Toronto, ON M5A 2K7

Canada

(888) 204-7777

Website: http://www.egale.ca

Egale focuses on increasing equal rights and access to services for LGBTQ people throughout Canada. The organization provides youth resources, refugee services, information specifically targeted at indigenous two-spirit people, and more.

National Center for Transgender Equality

1400 16th Street, NW

Suite 510

Washington, DC 20036

(202) 652-4542

Website: http://www.transequality.org

The National Center for Transgender Equality is a US advocacy group for transgender people. They compile resources, provide legal services, perform nationwide studies, and advocate for trans rights on a policy level.

National Domestic Violence Hotline

PO Box 161810

Austin, TX 78716

(800) 799-7233

Website: www.thehotline.org

The National Domestic Violence Hotline provides those suffering domestic abuse from family, partners, or roommates with help throughout the United States. They can provide direct help for LGBTQ people and have links to other resources specifically targeted at queer-aligned people.

Organization for Refuge, Asylum & Migration

333 Valencia Street, #250

San Francisco, CA 94103

(415) 399-1701

Website: http://www.oramrefugee.org

The Organization for Refuge, Asylum, and Migration advocates for and protects vulnerable refugees, including LGBTQ refugees. They work with governments and international agencies to provide assistance, publications, and professional training aimed at helping refugees, asylum seekers, and migrants have safe and healthy lives.

Sylvia Rivera Law Project

147 W 24th Street, 5th Floor

New York, NY 10011

(212) 337-8550

Website: http://www.srlp.org

The Sylvia Rivera Law Project offers services aimed at making it easier for all people to self-determine their gender identity and expression, regardless of income or race. They provide prisoner advocacy, legal information, and more.

Trans Equality Society of Alberta

PO Box 2053 Edmonton Main

Edmonton, AB T5J 2P4

Canada

Website: http://www.tesaonline.org

Trans Equality Society of Alberta advocates for social justice and equality both in Alberta and all of Canada. They provide regular reports and resources, links to organizations throughout Canada and beyond, and discuss legal developments pertaining to transgender rights.

Transgender Law Center

PO Box 70976

Oakland, CA 94612

(510) 587-9696

Website: https://www.transgenderlawcenter.org

Transgender Law Center provides resources and education for transgender people and their allies. They are the largest transgender-led organization in the world and provide legal advice, assistance for immigrants and detainees, and other empowering services at no cost.

Trans Lifeline

2443 Fillmore Street, #380-9468

San Francisco, CA 94115

US: (877) 565-8860, CAN: (877) 330-6366

Website: https://www.translifeline.org

Trans Lifeline supports transgender and gender nonconforming people in times of crisis in the United States and Canada. They operate a 24/7 hotline for crisis assistance, whether that means suicidal ideations or something else.

Trans Youth Equality Foundation

PO Box 7441

Portland, ME 04112

(207) 478-4087

Website: http://www.trasnyouthequality.org

Trans Youth Equality Foundation provides education and support for transgender and gender non-conforming youth and their families. Their resources include documents aimed at health care professionals and parents, youth camps, book recommendations, and more.

The Trevor Project

PO Box 69232

West Hollywood, CA 90069

(310) 271-8845

Website: http://www.thetrevorproject.org

The Trevor Project is a US-based nonprofit that offers programs for LGBTQ youth in the United States, including education and resources along with a 24/7 crisis hotline, text line, and online chat service.

Websites

Because of the changing nature of internet links, Rosen Publishing has developed an online list of websites related to the subject of this book. This site is updated regularly. Please use this link to access the list:

http://www.rosenlinks.com/COP/dysphoria

For Further Reading

Coyote, Ivan E., and Rae Spoon. *Gender Failure*. Vancouver, BC: Arsenal Pulp Press, 2014.

Currah, Paisley, and Susan Stryker. *Transgender Studies Quarterly*. Volume 1, Number 1–2. Durham, NC: Duke University Press, 2014.

Erickson-Schroth, Laura. *Trans Bodies, Trans Selves: A Resource for the Transgender Community*. New York, NY: Oxford University Press, 2014.

Gino, Alex. *George*. New York, NY: Scholastic Press, 2015.

Hill, Katie R. *Rethinking Normal: A Memoir in Transition*. New York, NY: Simon & Schuster, 2014.

Mock, Janet. *Redefining Realness: My Path to Womanhood, Identity, Love & So Much More*. New York, NY: Atria Books, 2014.

Staley, Erin. *Defeating Stress and Anxiety*. New York, NY: Rosen Publishing, 2016.

Staley, Erin. *Laverne Cox*. New York, NY: Rosen Publishing, 2017.

Thompson, Tamara. *Transgender People*. New York, NY: Greenhaven Publishing, 2015.

Woods, Sara. *Identifying as Transgender*. New York, NY: Rosen Publishing, 2017.

Bibliography

Ahmed, Osman & Chai Jindasurat. *Lesbian, Gay, Bisexual, Transgender, Queer, and HIV-Affected Hate Violence in 2014.* New York, NY: New York City Anti-Violence Project, 2015.

American Psychiatric Association. "Gender Dysphoria in the DSM-5." Psychiatry.org. Retrieved January 18, 2017. https://psychiatry .org/File%20Library/Psychiatrists/Practice /DSM/APA_DSM-5-Gender-Dysphoria.pdf? _ga=1.226585630.2043484884.1484761912.

Boghani, Priyanka. "When Transgender Kids Transition, Medical Risks are Both Known and Unknown." PBS Frontline. June 30, 2015. http:// www.pbs.org/wgbh/frontline/article/when -transgender-kids-transition-medical-risks -are-both-known-and-unknown.

Cho, Stephanie, Carolyn Laub, Sean Saifa M. Wall, Chris Daley, and Courtney Joslin. *Beyond the Binary.* Oakland, CA: Genders & Sexualities Alliance Network, 2004.

Crenshaw, Kimberlé. *Demarginalizing the Intersection of Race and Sex: A Black Feminist Critique of Antidiscrimination Doctrine, Feminist Theory and Antiracist Politics.* University of Chicago Legal Forum: Vol. 1989: Iss. 1, Article 8. Chicago, IL: University of Chicago Legal Forum, 1989.

Flores, A. R., J. L. Herman, G. J. Gates, & T. N. T. Brown. *How Many Adults Identify as Transgender in the United States?* Los Angeles, CA: The Williams Institute, 2016.

Flores, A. R., T. N. T. Brown, & J. L. Herman. *Race and Ethnicity of Adults who Identify as Transgender in the United States.* Los Angeles, CA: The Williams Institute, 2016.

James, S. E., J. L. Herman, S. Rankin, M. Keisling, L. Mottet, & M. Ana. *The Report of the 2015 U.S. Transgender Survey.* Washington, DC: National Center for Transgender Equality, 2016.

Knudson, Gail, et. al. "Position Statement on Medical Necessity of Treatment, Sex Reassignment, and Insurance Coverage in the U.S.A." World Professional Association for Transgender Health, December 21, 2016. http://www.wpath .org/site_page.cfm?pk_association_webpage _menu=1352&pk_association_webpage=3947.

Lambda Legal. "FAQ: Equal Access to Health Care." Know Your Rights. Retrieved January 20, 2017. http://www.lambdalegal.org/know-your-rights /article/trans-related-care-faq.

Lambda Legal. "How Schools Can Support Transgender Students." Know Your Rights. Retrieved January 20, 2017. http://www .lambdalegal.org/know-your-rights/article /youth-tgnc-friendly-schools.

National Center for Transgender Equality. "Employment." Issues. Retrieved January 21, 2017. http://www.transequality.org/issues/employment.

O'Hara, Mary E. "Nation's First Known Intersex Birth Certificate Issued in NYC." NBC News. December 29, 2016. http://www.nbcnews.com/feature/nbc-out/nation-s-first-known-intersex-birth-certificate-issued-nyc-n701186.

Parekh, Ranna. "What is Gender Dysphoria." American Psychiatric Association. February 2016. https://psychiatry.org/patients-families/gender-dysphoria/what-is-gender-dysphoria?_ga=1.66113453.2043484884.1484761912.

Parry, Wynne. "Gender Dysphoria: DSM-5 Reflects Shift in Perspective On Gender Identity." LiveScience/The Huffington Post. June 4, 2013. http://www.huffingtonpost.com/2013/06/04/gender-dysphoria-dsm-5_n_3385287.html

Stearns, Amber. "Rep. Borders Courts Needless Controversy With Birth Certificate Bill." Nuvo. January 12, 2017. http://www.nuvo.net/Slash/archives/2017/01/12/rep-borders-courts-needless-controversy-with-birth-certificate-bill.

Tan, Yvette. "Miss Fa'afafine: Behind Samoa's 'Third Gender' Beauty Pageant." BBC News. September 1 2016. http://www.bbc.com/news/world-asia-37227803.

Transgender Law Center. "Facebook to Change Real Name Policy." Featured. December 16, 2016. https://transgenderlawcenter.org /archives/12326.

Trans People of Color Committee. "Addressing Anti-Transgender Violence: Exploring Realities, Challenges and Solutions." Human Rights Campaign. November 2015. http://www.hrc .org/resources/addressing-anti-transgender -violence-exploring-realities-challenges-and -sol.

U.S. Department of Homeland Security. "Policy Memorandum: Application of Immigration Benefits for Transgender Individuals; Addition of Adjudicator's Field Manual Subchapter 10.22 and Revisions to AFM Subchapter 21.3." U.S. Citizenship and Immigration Services. April 13, 2012. https://www.uscis.gov/sites/default/files /USCIS/Outreach/Feedback%20Opportunities /Interim%20Guidance%20for%20Comment /Transgender_FINAL.pdf.

About the Author

Ellen McGrody is an author and a transgender woman dedicated to shining a spotlight on the lives of transgender people. She founded Run for Our Rights, an annual gaming marathon benefitting the Transgender Law Center, and Good Lil' Trans Girl, a parody blog which tackles transmisogyny through humor. She lives with her fiancée and cat in Oakland, California.

About the Expert Reviewer

Dr. Jan Hittelman, a licensed psychologist with over thirty years experience working with children and families, has authored monthly columns for the Daily Camera, Boulder Valley School District, and online for the Rosen Publishing Group. He is the founder of the Boulder Counseling Cooperative and the director of Boulder Psychological Services.

Photo Credits

Cover Yagi Studio/Taxi Japan/Getty Images; p. 5 David Livingston/Getty Images; pp. 7, 12–13, 28, 32, 42–43, 54, 73, 77, 94 © AP Images; pp. 10–11, 68–69 New York Daily News/Getty Images; p. 17 Gideon Mendel/Corbis Historical/Getty Images; p. 21 llewellynchin/Shutterstock.com; p. 26 Ira Berger/Alamy Stock Photo; pp. 33, 92 Joe Amon/The Denver Post/Getty Images; pp. 37, 89 J. Bicking/Shutterstock.com; pp. 46–47 Kansas City Star/Tribune News Service/Getty Images; p. 50 Christine Hochkeppel/Worcester Telegram & Gazette/AP Images; p. 58 Alexander Walter/Photodisc/Getty Images; pp. 62–63 Chicago Tribune/Tribune News Service/Getty Images; pp. 66–67 Rawpixel.com/Shutterstock.com; p. 81 Rido/Shutterstock.com; p. 85 H.S. Photos/Alamy Stock Photo; pp. 90–91 The Boston Globe/Getty Images; back cover and interior pages background pattern © iStockphoto.com/Sergei Dubrovskii.

Designer: Nicole Russo-Duca; Photo Researcher: Nicole DiMella